CH

TU

Dante

▲ *Mural of a battle. Temple of the Jaguars, Chichen Itza.*

CONTENTS

▸ *Chac Mool.*

Chichen Itza
Uxmal
Kabah
Labna
Sayil
Xlapak
Coba
Tulum
MEXICO
Uaxactun
Palenque
Tikal
BELIZE
GUATEMALA
HONDURAS
Copan
EL SALVADOR

▲ *The Castle or Pyramid of Kukulcan: the most imposing structure at Chichen Itza.*

CHICHEN ITZA

CITY OF THE WISE MEN OF THE WATER

At the brim of the well where the Wise Men of the Water live: In the Maya language this is "Chichen Itza", name of one of the most important city-states in pre-Hispanic America. At the height of its development, this political and ceremonial enclave dominated a large part of the Maya territory today known as the Southern Lowlands and forming the peninsula of Yucatan.

The territory in which Chichen Itza and other Maya cities are located in the Yucatan Peninsula is flat, and covered with low jungle. Beneath this flat land are subterranean rivers which make the soil fertile. However, the land is porous and not conducive to the formation of surface lakes and rivers. To compensate, the underground currents form natural water deposits in caves, which are known as cenotes. The cenotes (a term which is derived from the Maya, *dzonot*) form one of the most important sources of water in the region, as they make it possible to acquire water during the dry season. The Maya also constructed artificial cisterns called *chultunes*. This assured them a continuous water supply.

According to the traditional history of the site, a group of Maya settled in the area now known as Old Chichen in the year 435 A. D. (Classical period). From 495 A. D. to about 625 A. D. the first settlers constructed buildings in the Chenes and Puuc styles.

In about 900 A. D. the Itza tribe arrived at Chichen bringing with them a new architectonic style characterized by severe building lines, and with ornamental motifs dominated by representations of the Serpent-God Kukulcan. This style was traditionally known as Maya-Toltec, because it was thought that a Nahuatl (Mexican) group had influenced the Itza.

Modern archaeologists are still trying to find out about the day to day practices of the Maya at Chichen Itza.

Only in recent times have they managed to sketch some aspects of the daily life of the men who built this important pre-Hispanic city.

◀ *The Castle or Pyramid of Kukulcan.*

Origin, splendor and decadence

It is likely that between 500 B. C. and 325 A. D. what we now call Old Chichen was a simple village of wood and thatch huts.

The people who founded that village evolved politically and socially to form a ruling class, around 325 A. D. Then, the Period of the Theocratic City began. Ruled by priests who worshipped the rain god Chaac, the inhabitants of Chichen Itza began to construct monuments close to the Xtoloc cenote.

With the domination by the Itza accomplished, the First Period of the Military City began, which was to last until 1185. During this period the new lords developed their culture in their newly won territory, to which they gave their name.

The ruling elite in Chichen Itza was comprised of warriors, priests and merchants.

The Itza introduced the cult of the god Kukulcan (the plumed serpent), equivalent to Quetzalcoatl in the Highlands of Mexico.

The architectural contributions of the Itza included buildings with sloping elevations and vertical walls, as well as abundant representations of the plumed-serpent god. The Itza practiced a phallic cult and beheaded prisoners of war.

Militarism can destroy entire civilizations, but in the case of the Itza this was without a doubt the very basis of their great culture. This is evident in the macabre Tzompantli or Platform of Skulls, a monument to the cruelty the Itza deployed, showing the skulls of hundreds of enemies impaled on the wall.

At the beginning of the XV century, Mayapan collapsed as a political center due to internal conflicts. The collapse must have affected the future of Chichen Itza, which was also deserted during this time. Later, this city was sporadically occupied for the celebration of some religious ceremonies, and then for many centuries it remained forgotten in the jungle.

▲ *Atlas figure in the Temple of the Warriors.*

Map of Chichen Itza Archaeological Site

Chichen Itza

1 The Sacred Cenote
2 The Ball Court
3 The Tzompantli
4 The Platform of the Eagles and Jaguars
5 The Venus Platform
6 The Castle
7 The Temple of the Warriors
8 The Market Place
9 The Steam Bath
10 The Thousand Columns Group
11 The Temple of the Large Tables
12 The Xtoloc Cenote
13 The Ossuary
14 The Chichanchob or Red House
15 The House of the Deer
16 The Caracol or Observatory
17 The Temple of Panels
18 The Nuns' House
19 The Church
20 The Akab Dzib

PLATE I - THE CASTLE OR PYRAMID OF KUKULCAN

North Group

The Castle or Pyramid of Kukulcan

One of the tallest and most remarkable examples of Maya architecture, it was built during the high point of the Itza-Cocom culture, during the decadence of Mayapan.

It is a four sided pyramid, with a rectangular temple on the top.

If one stops to think about it, it is a little unsettling to find that the Maya-called the Greeks of America-could have designed such frugal architecture, almost the enemy of ornamentation. However, amidst the somberness of the Castle exists an austere and fearful esthetic project, and a concept

▼ *The pyramid is 79 feet tall, and is set on a rectangular platform 197 feet wide. The nine stepped levels or sections represent the symbolic number of the Underworld (the Maya hell).*

◄ *The façade on the lower half of the temple is plain and undecorated. The doorjambs at each entrance conserve bas-reliefs representing richly dressed personages with elaborate headdresses.*

of beauty inspired in the bellicose people who dominated those lands.

The principal façade of this temple has two columns representing serpents with open jaws. These form the main entrance, topped with a large mask of the god Chaac. The principal entrance has a lintel sustained by two square pillars, adorned with bas-reliefs.

▼ *Stone balustrades flank each staircase. The northern balustrades originate from two feathered serpent's heads, forming huge effigies of the god Kukulcan.*

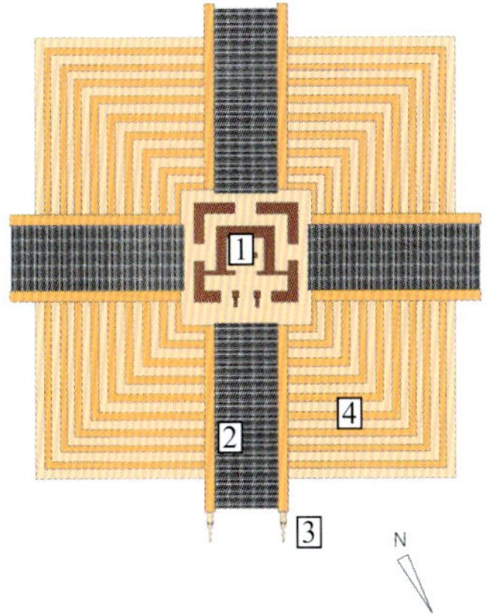

The Castle

1 Upper Temple
2 Great Staircase
3 Serpents' Heads
4 Superimposed stages

Substructure of the Castle

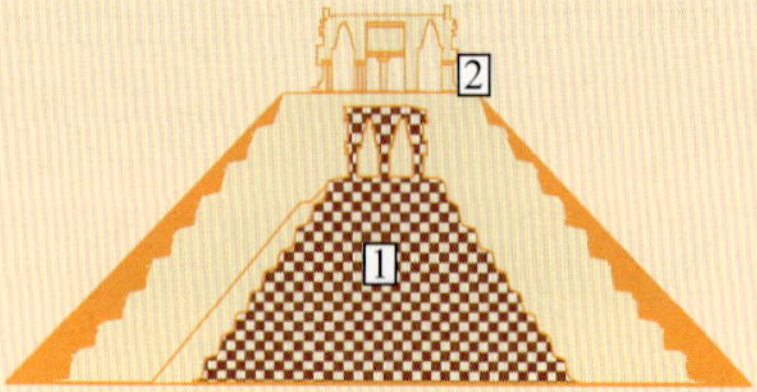

1 First structure
2 Present building

The Kukulcan pyramid was built on top of an earlier, smaller structure, which it covered. During the excavations the archaeologists discovered the smaller temple, which is 16 meters high.

▼ *Throne in the form of a jaguar.*

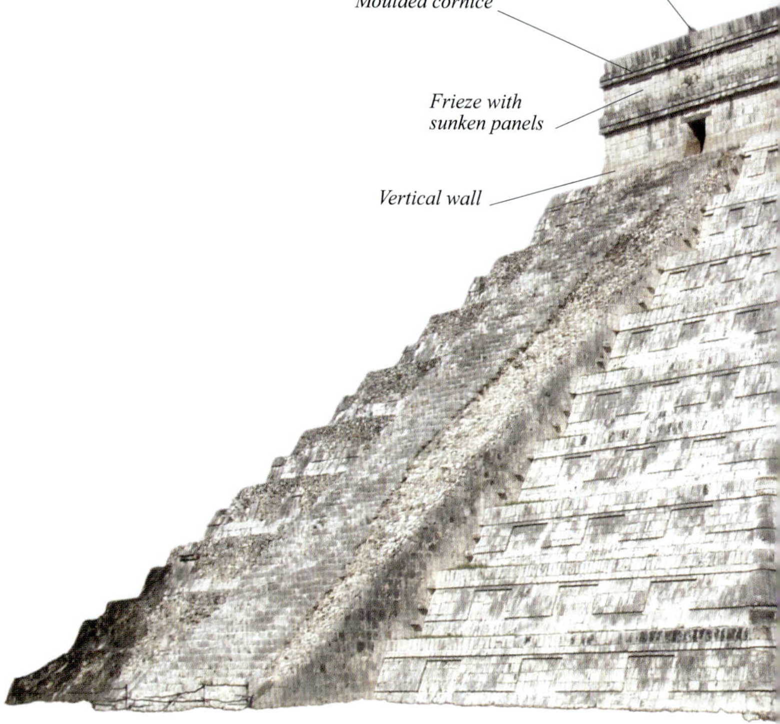

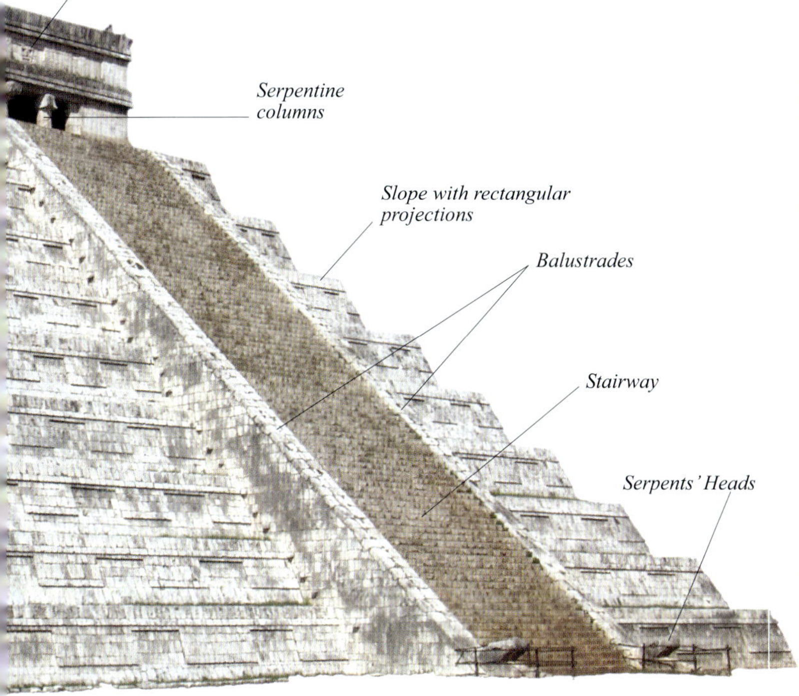

The descent of Kukulcan

The Light and Shadow Phenomenon. Testimony to the amazing advance of the Maya in architecture and astronomy is the "light and shadow" phenomenon that takes place on the northern staircase of the Castle during the Spring Equinox (21st March) and the Autumn Equinox (21st September). About three o'clock in the afternoon on the days of the equinox the sun projects seven triangles of light onto the balustrade on the northeastern side of the Castle. These begin to move up and down along the balustrade to form the silhouette of a serpent.

▼ *For the pre-Hispanic Maya "the descent of Kukulcán" probably marked the start of the agricultural cycle. The phenomenon draws thousands of visitors each year.*

"... southeast from this rises the Castillo..., the first building which we saw, and from every point of view the grandest and most conspicuous object that towers above the plain... At the foot... are two colossal serpents' heads... with mouths open and tongues protruding."

John Stephens / Incidents of Travel in Yucatan - *Engraving by Frederick Catherwood.*

▼ *The ancient buildings around the Great Esplanade at Chichen Itza greet the visitor with overwhelming monumentality.*

▲ *The Castle, seen from the Venus Platform.*

▶ *On each side of the pyramid is a large staircase leading to the temple above.*

The Ball Game

The Ball Game is characteristic of Mesoamerican societies. The Ball Game was more a ceremonial ritual than a sport and probably represented the symbolic recreation of the mythical combat between night and day. There is a singular acoustic phenomenon peculiar to the Ball Game Court: if one speaks in the Temple in the southern end the voice can be heard at the opposite end, as the sound reverberates along the walls of the North Temple.

▲ In total, the complex with its two annexed temples to north and south measures 551 feet long by 230 feet wide.

▼ The bas-reliefs on the side benches show players from two teams around a ball bearing the symbol of death.

▼ The stone rings set into the central part of each wall are also distinctive for the beautiful, tooled decoration.

▼ The distinctive features of the South Temple are six fragments of pillars that rise up from the base. These square based pillars, decorated with figures of warriors, suapport the entrance to the temple. Set on one of the pillars is a square panel showing the figure of Kukulcan coming out of the jaws of a serpent.

PLATE II - THE TEMPLE OF JAGUARS IN THE BALL COURT

The Rules of the Game

It has only been possible to partially reconstruct the rules of the ball game, thanks to pictorial representations and stone monuments. We know that at the beginning of the game the ball was thrown onto the court by hand, and that from that moment it could only be touched with the hips and thighs. We do not known the number of players, the scoring system, or how the winner was decided; according to information in the Popol Vuh we can infer that the game could be played one on one, in pairs, or in teams. In the depictions, the players appear in various attitudes, showing the different plays in this contest.

▼ Ball game showing a critical moment in the game. The depiction corresponds to the late classical period, 600-900 AD.

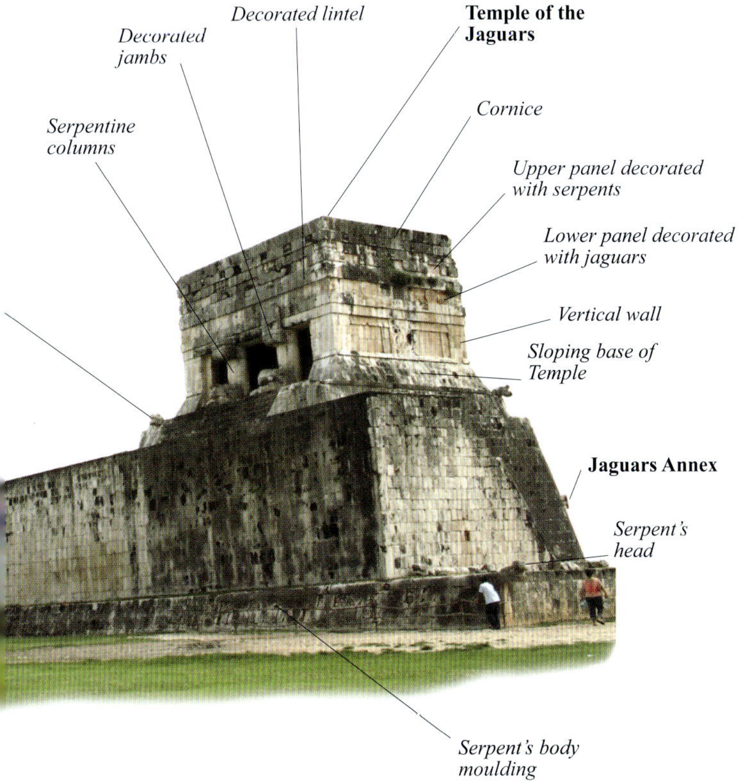

The ball

The ball for the game was made from liquid latex extracted from rubber trees. When heated, the resin formed threads that were first rolled up and then squeezed by hand or pressed in a mould.

The weight of the ball varied between 3 and 5 kilos, and when it became deformed it had to be stretched back into shape.

Each player had his own ball as part of his personal equipment.

In the depictions, there are some balls small enough to fit in the hand, and others bigger than a soccer ball.

▼ *Ball game between two rulers. Late classical period, Toniná, Chiapas.*

"... (there) are two massive stone rings... On the rim and border were two sculptured entwined serpents. I shall call (this structure) the Gymnasium or Tennis-court."

John Stephens / Incidents of Travel in Yucatan - *Engraving by Frederick Catherwood.*

The Temple of the Jaguars

The Temple of the Jaguars was built on the east wall of the Ball Game. An interesting mosaic repeats along the length of the frieze: two jaguars advance, from different directions, towards a round shield. The upper tableau is filled in with the bodies of two plumed serpents, with their heads at the edges of the frieze and the tails interlocked in the center.

▶ *The Annexe to the Temple of the Jaguars is located at the rear of the Temple itself and comprises a single room with a vaulted ceiling. Two stone pilasters support the entrance, creating three access ways.*

◀ *The bases of the columns are imposing serpents' heads. On the walls of these rooms, some mural paintings are preserved.*

▼ *Two solid columns form the entrance to the temple, sculpted in the form of plumed serpents.*

▼ *The North Temple was the first temple at Chichen Itza to use the sloping elevation and vertical wall.*

The Tzompantli

The structure is a large platform whose most notable detail is the collocation of the skulls in the bas-relief decoration which gives the structure its name: the Platform of the Skulls. The base is sustained by three tableaux decorated with skulls and divided by mouldings.

This is the monument that gives the clearest testimony to the practice of human sacrifice, carried out for religious-military ends, by the rulers of Chichen Itza.

▼ *Tzompantli, in the Nahua language, means "wall of skulls".*

▲ *Hypothetical reconstruction of the Tzompantli at Chichén Itzá.*
The central tableau is wider and has two lines of skulls.

◄ *The salient east limb has representations of eagles and warriors who carry human heads in their hands.*

► *The bodies of serpents crown the structure.*

The Platform of the Eagles and Jaguars

This is a small platform with four stairways. On the base of the structure there is a vertical wall with raised panels displaying images which relate to the course of the sun across the sky during the day and its descent to the underworld at night, as "Sun of the Earth". The eagles and jaguars symbolize the warriors who capture victims to feed the sun god.

◄ *The balustrades end in cubes or blocks out of which rise the serpents' heads.*

▲ *On the raised panels the Maya artisans carved the figures of jaguars devouring human hearts.*

PLATE III - THE PLATFORM OF THE EAGLES AND JAGUARS

◄ *The serpents' heads, set into cubes or blocks, finish off the balustrades.*

The Venus Platform

This is a square platform with stairways on each side. On the raised panels there are bas-reliefs of the planet Venus in the form of a "knot" of years, beside a half flower with asps on the petals, and the shape of the plaited mat (*pop* in Maya) as the symbol of power. In the recessed space Venus is depicted with jaguar claws emerging from the jaws of a plumed serpent.

▲ *The stone bas-reliefs still conserve traces of red, blue and yellow paint which heightened the representation of the morning star, the Bee-Star that the Maya observed with special fascination.*

▶ *The tableaux on the cornice show plumed serpents in motion, with fishes set inbetween the waves that are formed by the serpents' moving bodies.*

▼ *Reconstruction of the Platform of Venus.*

The Temple of the Warriors

The Temple of the Warriors is a structure 40 feet high and 133 feet wide. The central temple shows reliefs of warriors and eagles and jaguars devouring human hearts as well as representations of the god Tlalchitonatiuh.

The western staircase has stone balustrades, carved in the form of the bodies of plumed serpents and topped by two serpents' heads.

▼ The Temple of the Warriors seen from the top of the pyramid of Kukulcan.

▶ The twelve pilasters at the entrance to the Temple were decorated with figures of gods and warriors.

The Tomb of the Chac Mool

This substructure is conserved inside the basement of the Temple of the Warriors. Inside was a statue of Chac Mool wearing a type of helmet and a belt from which are hanging human heads. It must be pointed out that the name "Chac Mool" is not Maya: it was invented by the American explorer Augustus Le Plongeon.

► *The staircase provides access to an esplanade on which the upper temple is built. Set in front of this temple is the noteworthy statue of the Chac Mool, in-between two magnificent pillars in the form of serpents, with the heads at the base and the tails at the top.*

► *The upper temple of the Warriors is a nearly square structure containing two parallel areas. The central entrance is flanked by two vertical, carved strings of Chaac masks. On each side of these carvings there is a large mask of the god Kukulcan, emerging from the jaws of a plumed serpent.*

◀◀ The shape of the sloping base panel of the Temple of the Warriors has antecedents in the Temple of Tlahuizilapantecutli in the city of Tula.

◀ Mayan artists carved figures of eagles on the panels.

▶ Decorated pilaster in the Temple of the Warriors.

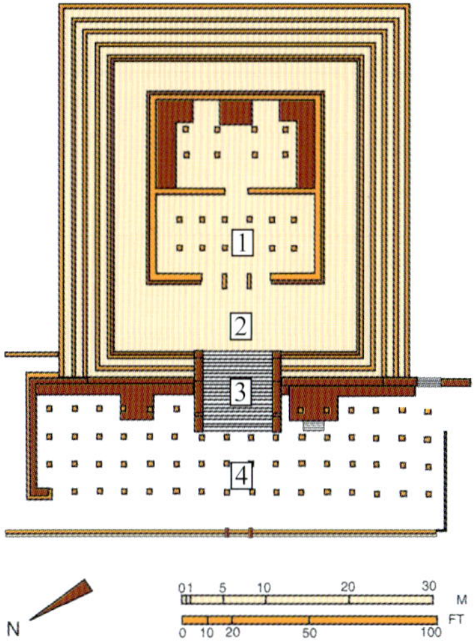

Temple of the Warriors

1 Upper temple
2 Esplanade
3 Stairway
4 Entrance pilasters

▶ The Temple of the Warriors shows Toltec influence in the grand colonnades which shield the base of the staircase and extend to the front and sides of the temple, connecting with the Thousand Columns Group.

▶ Hypothetical reconstruction of the Temple of the Warriors.

The Thousand Columns Group

This is a vast quadrangle. On the west side one can see the remains of four chambers, two of which were filled in so as to support a second floor. The columns were built between 900 A. D. and 1200 A.D. and show the remains of stucco covering, which would have been painted in different colors. Also, the colonnade supported a frieze of masks of Chaac and round shields.

The Southeast Colonnade has a large space with vaulted roofing, supported by the columns. The function of this area changed continually.

◄ *One of the most interesting elements of the group known as the Thousand Columns is the Northeast Colonnade, which is a structure in the form of a right angle.*

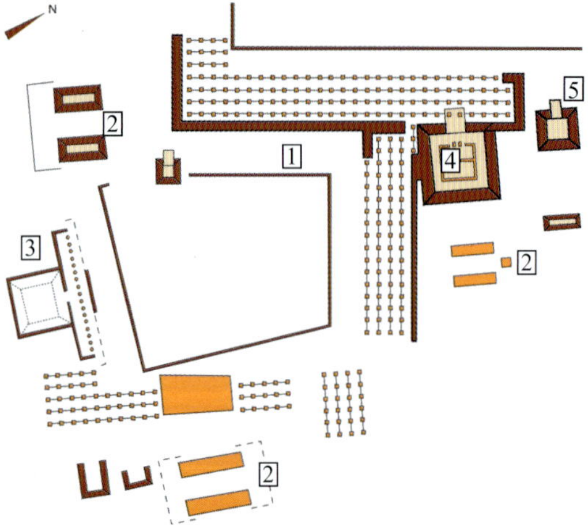

The Thousand Columns Group

1 The Thousand Columns Group
2 Ball Game
3 The Market Place
4 The Temple of the Warriors
5 The Temple of the Large Tables

PLATE IV - THE THOUSAND COLUMNS GROUP

The Market Place

The building traditionally known as the Market Place is set upon a platform 266 feet long and 49 feet wide. It has a central staircase with balustrades and a line of round pillars alternating with square pillars. These supported the arched roof, the widest in the city. A central door leads on to a square inner patio, 56 feet long each side, enclosed by the tallest columns of the area.

When it rained the water from the roof drained out through a carved stone drainage channel. Along the length of the walls there is a long bench, with the back sloped against the walls. It has not been proven that this area, today called the Market Place, really was a space used for trade and commerce.

◄ *Remains of the inner square patio, formed by the tallest columns in the area.*

▸ *Present state of one of the access gateways to the market, shown in reconstruction below.*

▸▸ *The Thousand Columns group and the Market Place date from the second period of the Military City, between 1200 and 1350. The group of columns on the north side is a little later.*

The restored friezes in the Market Place and in the Thousand Columns Group introduce a new type of decoration into this severe northern section of Chichen Itza, less threatening than the sacred serpents and the blood-thirsty jaguars that so clearly marked out the distinguished personages carved onto the walls of the Temple of the Jaguars.

▸ *Ideal reconstruction of one of the gateways to the Market at Chichen Itza.*

The Sacred Cenote

The Cenote is a naturally formed open well whose diameter from north to south is 165 feet, and from east to west, 200 feet. As part of the cult offered to the water god the pre-Hispanic Maya made ceremonial offerings, throwing into the well many precious objects. Later, they introduced the practice of making human sacrifices. The victims were warriors, children and maidens thrown to the bottom of the cenote. To one side of the south bank of the well they built some platforms on two levels, which perhaps were used as seats for those who witnessed the ceremonies. Beside this one can see the ruins of a building that was adapted into a steam bath or *temazcal*, where it is supposed that the victims were purified. Placed against this building is another platform that hangs over the edge of the cenote, from which the offerings would have been made.

◄ *The depth of the cenote is approximately 66 feet. The water is a greenish color due to the algae and micro organisms that breed there, and also due to the vegetation that surrounds the well.*

◄ *Ideal reconstruction of the steam bath at Chichen Itza, after a drawing by Tatiana Proskouriakoff.*

▼ *The bath had drainage tubing, and had openings in the upper part of the walls to provide ventilation and let out the steam.*

The Steam Bath

The steam bath still conserves part of the flat roof, as well as the remains of four columns in the portico and some stone slab seats placed against the façade. A narrow opening gives access to the inside, where there are stone slabs for the bathers to sit on. At the back there is a stove where stones were heated, onto which cold water was poured to producc steam.

▲ *Large serpents' heads finish off the balustrades of the Ossuary.*

◄ *It measures more than 33 feet high and appears to be a smaller replica of The Castle.*

▲ *The Ossuary pyramid forms a group of monuments that connect to the Xtoloc cenote.*

▼ *Near the pyramid stood the only stele known at Chichén Itzá.*

Central Group

The Ossuary or High Priest's Temple

This is a pyramid with nine stepped blocks and with a staircase on each of the four sides, with balustrades carved with interlocking serpents that lead to a temple at the top, whose entrance proudly displays two serpent columns.

The pyramid was built above a deep and extensive cavern, which one can descend to from the opening made in the floor of the temple above. At the entrance to the cavern there are seven tombs which contained jade, rock crystal, shell and copper offerings.

◄ *Closing off the quadrangle formed by the Chichanchob and the House of the Deer, at the far edge of the square and hidden amongst the trees and scrub are the remains of other structures that perhaps were temples, similar in structure to those still standing.*

▼ *The house of the deer must have been similar to the Chichanchob, but more than half of the structure has collapsed.*

The House of the Deer

This building is now very much destroyed. It must have been similar to the Chichanchob, but more than half of the structure has collapsed.

Above the roof the remains of the crest are barely conserved. The name of the temple, according to tradition, comes from a painting of a deer in the interior, that has now disappeared. From what remains to be seen today it seems possible that the building suffered from a water tract that washed away the stucco from the walls, where this painting might have been.

The Chichanchob or Red House

The Chichanchob is set on a rectangular platform with rounded corners. A stairway without balustrades provides access to the temple at the top, which has a flat façade adorned at the top with two crests, one at the front and one on the central part of the roof. The front crest is decorated with alternating fret patterns and masks of Chaac above the entrances. The style of the building corresponds to that of the Puuc Region.

▲ *The name The Red House is due to the red painting on the wide fresco or dado at the base of the façade.*

◄ *The front crest is of later construction than the one in the middle of the roof, which is ornamented with fret patterns in between two moldings, and with openings in the base. The name Chichanchob (Small Holes) perhaps comes from the small openings in the original crest in the middle of the roof.*

PLATE V - THE CHICHANCHOB

The Caracol or Observatory

This building, one of the few circular structures built by the Maya, is believed to have been used for astronomical observations, through openings in the top of the tower.

The so-called Caracol or Observatory is a structure built in the form of a large circular tower set on a platform with a central staircase. The base is set on another rectangular platform, decorated with a cornice of rounded corners on the upper part. The Caracol (whose form is similar to that of modern observatories) is really built of three superimposed buildings.

◄ *View of the astronomical observatory known as the "Snail", with its buildings attached to the main platform.*

The first part of the cylindrical tower is formed by two concentric walls which enclose a pair of circular chambers each with four doorways.
The second level comprises the cornice of the first level and a second, narrower one, which frames a frieze. Above one of the doors, the frieze has a mask of Chaac and a seated figure, framed with motifs made of feathers and serpents.
The third and fourth parts of the tower have deteriorated, but a series of openings or windows can still be glimpsed which perhaps served for making astronomical observations.

◄ *The small windows at the top of the tower, which may have been used for astronomical observations, gave this building the name of the Observatory.*

▲ *The circular tower, standing on a circular base 36 ft in diameter, has a first section made up of two concentric walls enclosing two inner chambers, each with four doors.*

▲ *Staircase from the main base of the Snail, with serpents' heads at the ends of the lateral inclines.*

◄ *Here the Mayan priests studied the cosmos and formulated predictions for the daily life of the people.*

On the west side of the larger base there is a staircase whose balustrades are adorned with intertwining serpents' heads.
The total height of the monument is 75 feet. The structure was constructed during the first period of the Military City.

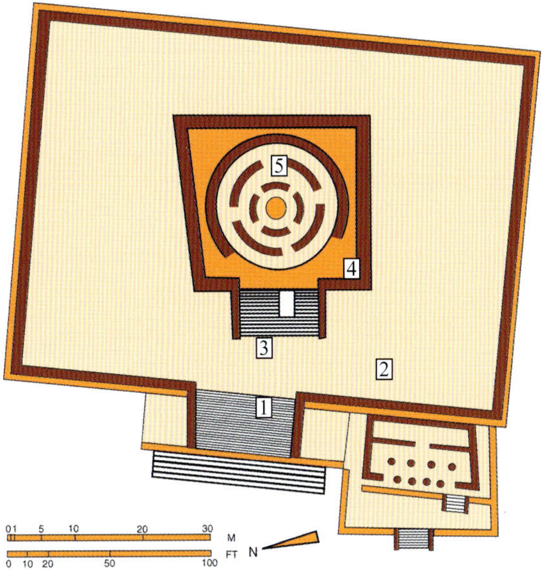

The Observatory

1 Staircase
2 Rectangular Platform
3 Central Staircase
4 Platform
5 Circular Tower

▶ *One of the names of the monument, The Observatory, comes from the supposed function of the building. The other name comes from the spiral staircase set at the heart of the building.*

Mayan Astronomy

The Maya studied the sun, the moon and Venus, and their observations included some visible bodies such as Mercury, Mars and other stars. Their priests, the greatest astronomers of the time, succeeded in calculating solar and lunar eclipses, the rising and setting of Venus and the movements of stars and planets, as well as the solar year, with great accuracy.

Even today, scientists are amazed at the development of Mayan astronomy. For the ancient Maya, astronomy and cosmogony were closely linked in their mythical conception of the universe.

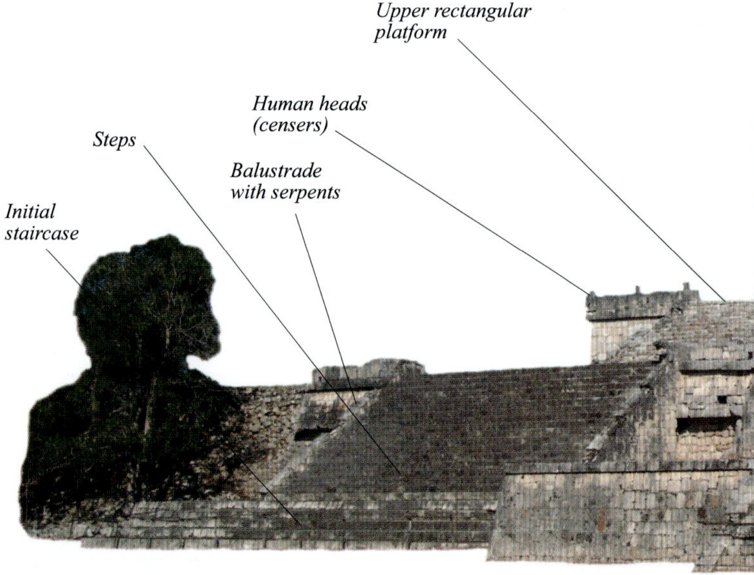

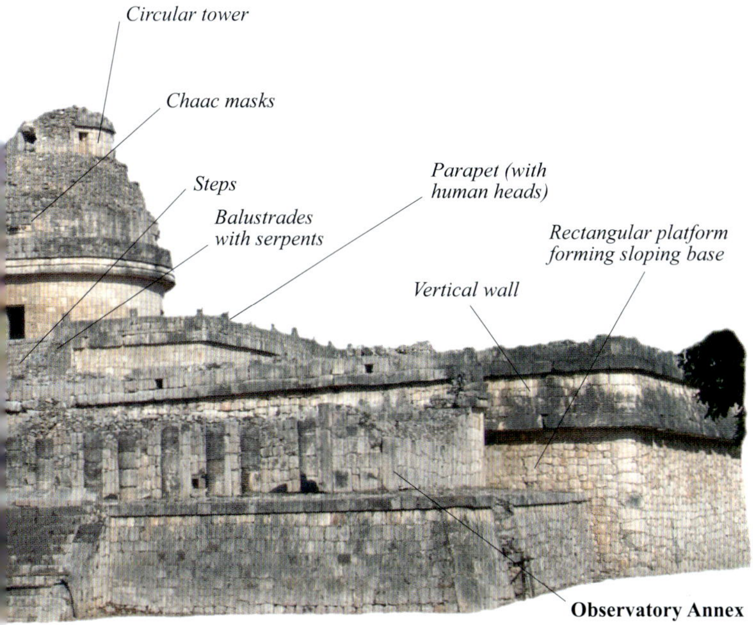

The Lords of Time

Known as "The Lords of Time", the Maya were unique in elevating to the rank of gods not only the idea of time, but also the periods into which it is divided. They represented time as supernatural beings whose mission was to maintain order in the universe. The Mayan gods of time completed their life cycle in a constant circular movement beginning with their birth, developing with the manifestation of their characteristics, and finishing with their death. They were then re-born and a new cycle of birth and death was begun.

"... we reach... the edifice conspicuous among the ruins of Chichen for its picturesque appearance... and when entire, even among the great buildings around, this structure must have presented a striking appearance."

John Stephens / Incidents of Travel in Yucatan - *Engraving by Frederick Catherwood.*

PLATE VI - THE CARACOL OR OBSERVATORY

"(...) it is remarkable for its good state of preservation, and the richness and beauty of its ornaments.(...) It has two cornices of tasteful and elaborate design."

John Stephens / Incidents of Travel in Yucatan - *Drawing by Frederick Catherwood.*

The East Annex of the Nunnery

This structure has the most beautiful frieze in Chichen Itza, with a vast number of masks of the god Chaac on the sides. All the façades of the Annex are decorated, in keeping with the Chenes style.

The principal façade has a frieze displaying masks of Chaac on either side of a central medallion above the entrance. Set onto this is a sculpted figure in stucco, with a head-dress of beautiful feather and fret patterns.

◀ *Reconstruction of the East Annex to the Nuns' Building.*

▼ *The architectural styles of these structures derive from the Chenes and Puuc areas, in which the façade was decorated with mosaics and panels with latticework or geometric designs.*

▲ *Personage with feathered headdress in the central medallion on the east Annex to Nuns' Building.*

▶ *East Annex of the Nuns' group. Behind is the Nuns' Building itself.*

The Nuns' House

This is one of the most imposing of all the architectural groups in Chichen Itza.

The main façade of the complex faces north, and comprises three buildings: the Nuns', the East Annex and the Southeast Annex. The three date from different periods of construction.

The Nuns' Building stood on a base that is now no longer visible; the main section of the building is 33 ft high, with a central staircase on the north side, which led to the upper temple. The temple has a profusely decorated façade, in the Chenes style.

◄ *Main façade of the Nuns' group, with its wide staircase leading to the upper temple.*

To the left of the tall, heavy structure is the square building called The Church, with the Annex of the Nunnery, and a small Ball Court. Owing to the great number of rooms that divide the upper temples the explorers during the Colonial Period believed that the building would have served as a cloister for the training of priestesses.

▲ *The Nuns' House was probably a civic-ceremonial center during the rule of the priests in Old Chichen.*

▲ *In all, the monument measures 165 feet in length, 75 feet in width and 54 feet in height.*

▼ *The Nuns' group, after a drawing by Federick Catherwood.*

The Church

This square building, with a crest on the roof, has one single vaulted room. The façade displays a profuse and symmetrical ornamentation of stone mosaic in the upper part and beneath, a mouding of stepped fret shapes. Next, comes the frieze with a mask of Chaac in the middle. To either side are niches containing the figures of four *bacabes* or "supporters of the sky",

◄ *It is probable that the building served for paying homage to the gods of rain and water, because of the many masks of Chaac used in its decoration.*

depicted as an armadillo, a sea-snail, a turtle and a crab. In the corners to either side of these are masks of Chaac. Next, there is a figure in the form of a serpent between two mouldings. Above all this is a crest with a further band of fret patterns between two mouldings, on top of which are three more masks of Chaac.

▶ *The corners of the Church are finished with imposing masks of Chaac, the rain god.*

▼ *The center of the frieze on the façade is decorated with the figure of a Chaac mask.*

◄ *The Church Building was in good condition when Catherwood drew it in 1842.*

▼ *Side view of the Church. The enormous noses of the god Chaac stand out from the decorated frieze. In the background, part of the Nuns' group.*

PLATE VII - THE CHURCH

The Akab Dzib

The Akab Dzib consists of one central building and two rooms. Later two buildings were annexed, each with eight rooms. The three groups are roofed with the Maya vault or false arch. In total the three buildings have eighteen rooms.
The east façade shows some blocks or seats of well-cut stone.

▲ *On the lintel of one of the inner doorways there is an engraving of a priest seated on a throne before a type of stove. He is surrounded by hieroglyphic symbols that have not been deciphered. The difficulty of deciphering the symbols on the building has givent it its name, as in Maya Akab Dzib means "obscure writing".*

► *Inside some of the rooms there are handprints in red paint on the walls. These perhaps refer to Kabul (the Celestial Hand or Creator), the Maya god of the celestial bower.*

South Group

The southern group belongs to old Chichén and is a complex of buildings located in the jungle, to the south of the group made up by the Observatory and the Nunnery. The buildings of the southern group were constructed between the 7th and 10th centuries AD and correspond to the Puuc architectural style. The most important are the Temples of the First Series, of the Phalluses, of the Owls and of the Atlases.

▼ *Discoveries show that the Temple of the First Series covers an earlier structure belonging to the first period of the Theocratic City. The lintel has engravings of calendar hieroglyphs that form the only complete inscription to be found in the Chichen Itza ruins. Thus its archaeological value is tremendous.*

▶ *The buildings of old Chichén, or the southern group, belong to an earlier phase of the city, when it was inhabited by people of the Puuc region.*

▲ *Temple of the Wind at Tulum.*

TULUM

A particularly evocative and inspiring case is this city rising proudly on the shores of the Mexican Caribbean. The precinct, which is unusual among Mayan sites in being surrounded by walls, contains around 60 structures. The city, which was originally called Zamá, experienced a temporary rebirth for the Maya of Quintana Roo during the Caste Wars in the mid-19th century.

Tulum means "wall, castle, enclosure or fence". Apparently, Tulum is the only city of the region which has conserved its walls up to the present day.

The city rises up from a rocky wavelashed cliff. In design it is a rectangular quadrangle enclosed at the sides and front by the wall, and to the rear by the cliffs.

Unlike other great cities, the pyramids at Tulum are small and not as imposing or impressive as those of other Mayan settlements.

However, the impression which the visitor receives is that of finding oneself in a city "made to measure, for man's pleasure", owing to the surrounding beautiful beaches.

◄ *The Castle occupies the highest point in the city, and dominates both the walled precinct and the cliffs.*

The Castle

In the year 1518, the conquistador Juan de Grijalba referred to Tulum as a city "as big as Seville", with a tower "bigger than any he had seen". This last was undoubtedly the main structure of the walled city. In the upper part, interrupting the frieze, were three niches containing stucco figures, the central one of which is the Descending God, portrayed frequently at Tulum.

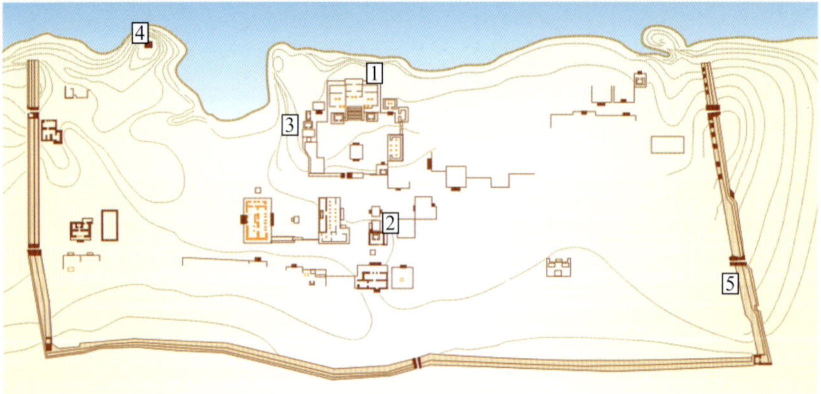

Tulum

1 The Castle
2 Temple of the Frescoes
3 Temple of the Descending God
4 Temple of the Wind
5 Wall

Temple of the Descending God

The Temple of the Descending God is dedicated to a deity linked to the setting sun, rain, lightning and also bee-keeping, for which reason he has also been called Ah Mucen Cab, the Bee God.

◄ *The main façade dominates the east side of the Interior Precinct, while the rear wall rises majestically from the edge of a cliff overlooking the Caribbean.*

► *Temple of the Descending God. This is a small temple dedicated to the Descending God.*

►► *The Temple of the Descending God, as it was when discovered by the explorers Stephens and Catherwood in 1842. Drawing by Catherwood.*

"... we had around us what we wanted at all the other places, the magnificence of nature. Clearing away the platform in front, we looked over an immense forest; walking around the moulding of the wall, we looked out upon the boundless ocean..."

John Stephens / Incidents of Travel in Yucatan - *Engraving by Frederick Catherwood.*

PLATE VIII - VIEW OF TULUM

► *House of the Halach Uinic. The name means "house of the great lord".*

▼ *The Temple of the Wind, surrounded by arid, stony ground, was dedicated to Kukulcan in his manifestation as God of the Wind.*

▼ *The illustration of this temple at Tulum, located in front of the Temple of the Frescoes, shows the enormous effort required to free the monuments from the surrounding jungle. The figure on the right is thought to be a self-portrait of Catherwood.*

▲ *The Temple of the Frescoes, as seen by Catherwood. The paintings in the Temple of Frescoes caused a profound impression on the explorers Stephens and Catherwood, who were reaffirmed in their opinion of the grandeur of the Mayan people.*

The Temple of Frescoes

The Temple of Frescoes owes its name to the mural paintings found on the building, representing deities framed by serpents, alligators, fish and other marine life, in what appears to be a religious ceremony dedicated to Kukulcan.

▶ *Temple of the Frescoes. It is located approximately in the center of the city, and is the most interesting and best-preserved building at Tulum.*

▶ *The inner walls of the Temple of Frescoes are decorated with elegant paintings of mythological subjects.*

▲ *Xaibe Palace.*

COBA

Considered the largest and one of the oldest pre-Hispanic cities in the northwest of Yucatan, the mysterious city of Coba is located a little over 31 miles from the coastal city of Tulum. Its name means "Water of the chachalacas (a kind of parrot)" and it is surrounded by jungle vegetation and five beautiful lakes (two of which are called Coba and Macanxoc).

It is also communicated with other Mayan cities by an interesting network of over 40 roads or *sacbés*, interlinked by means of an extraordinary feat of civil engineering. One of them, 62 miles long, reaches as far as Yaxcuná, which is only 12 miles from Chichen Itza. One of the principal architectonic features of Coba is the large number of stelae which contain calendar dates permitting us to fix the date of its foundation to 600 AD and assume occupation until the 15th century.

It is known that at its zenith, Cobá dominated a vast area, and engaged in wars with Chichen Itza to preserve its power and autonomy.

However, despite its importance, the city is not as beautiful as Uxmal or as imposing as Chichen Itza. The reason is the era: it is very old, and architectural styles had not developed.

▲ *The Paintings Group is the third complex visible at Coba, including three structures and thirteen altars, with a score of buildings in total.*

▼ *The group belongs to the last period of pre-Hispanic occupation at Cobá and shows several of the architectural and pictorial features of the so-called "East Coast" style, which is found for example at Tulum.*

◄ *The Xaibe Palace is also called Xaibé or Xai Be (xai "crossing" and be "road": "crossroads"). It is a building around which four sacbés come together, creating a kind of "meeting point", which may also have had mystical and religious significance.*

▼ *The Ball Court is built onto the corner of the biggest structure at Cobá, known as the Acropolis, a magnificent two-stage platform which appears to be merely a base. Remains of straw huts were found on it, but no stone buildings.*

◄ *Nohoch Mul Pyramid. One of the highest ancient Mayan structures in northeast Yucatan, its name means "large hill", a fitting name given its 138 ft. height.*

▼ *This large pyramid has seven levels with rounded corners.*

▼ *The façade still has two of three original niches which contain representations of the Descending God.*

▲ *The pyramid has a single temple at its top similar to those at Tulum.*

CHICHEN ITZA,

TULUM AND COBA.

1st edition 2007, Merida, Yucatan
ISBN: 970-605-395-6

Editorial Dante S. A. de C. V.
Calle 19 No. 102 x 20. Col. México.
C.P. 97125. Mérida, Yucatán. México.

Creative control: Javier Covo Torres.
Layout: Alejandra Cárdenas A., Laura Morales E.
Technical revisión: Laura Morales E.
Texts: Archivo Dante.
Translation: David Phillips.
Photography: David Baeza B.

PRINTED IN CHINA.